I0409631

FEDERAL GUIDELINES FOR DAM SAFETY:
EMERGENCY ACTION PLANNING
FOR DAM OWNERS

prepared by the
INTERAGENCY COMMITTEE ON DAM SAFETY

U. S. DEPARTMENT OF HOMELAND SECURITY
FEDERAL EMERGENCY MANAGEMENT AGENCY
OCTOBER 1998

Reprinted April 2004

PREFACE

In April 1977, President Carter issued a memorandum directing the review of federal dam safety activities by an *ad hoc* panel of recognized experts. In June 1979, the *ad hoc* interagency committee on dam safety (ICODS) issued its report, which contained the first guidelines for federal agency dam owners. The Federal Guidelines for Dam Safety (Guidelines) encourage strict safety standards in the practices and procedures employed by federal agencies or required of dam owners regulated by the federal agencies. The Guidelines address management practices and procedures but do not attempt to establish technical standards. They provide the most complete and authoritative statement available of the desired management practices for promoting dam safety and the welfare of the public.

To supplement the Guidelines, ICODS prepared and approved federal guidelines in the areas of emergency action planning; earthquake analysis and design of dams; and selecting and accommodating inflow design floods for dams. These publications, based on the most current knowledge and experience available, provided authoritative statements on the state of the art for three important technical areas involving dam safety. In 1994, the ICODS Subcommittee to Review/Update the Federal Guidelines began an update to these guidelines to meet new dam safety challenges and to ensure consistency across agencies and users. In addition, the ICODS Subcommittee on Federal/Non-Federal Dam Safety Coordination developed a new guideline, Hazard Potential Classification System for Dams.

With the passage of the National Dam Safety Program Act of 1996, Public Law 104-303, ICODS and its Subcommittees were reorganized to reflect the objectives and requirements of Public Law 104-303. In 1998, the newly convened Guidelines Development Subcommittee completed work on the update of all of the following guidelines:

- Federal Guidelines for Dam Safety: Emergency Action Planning for Dam Owners

- Federal Guidelines for Dam Safety: Hazard Potential Classification System for Dams

- Federal Guidelines for Dam Safety: Earthquake Analyses and Design of Dams

- Federal Guidelines for Dam Safety: Selecting and Accommodating Inflow Design Floods for Dams

- Federal Guidelines for Dam Safety: Glossary of Terms

The publication of these guidelines marks the final step in the review and update process. In recognition of the continuing need to enhance dam safety through coordination and information exchange among federal and state agencies, the Guidelines Development Subcommittee will be responsible for maintaining these documents and establishing additional guidelines that will help achieve the objectives of the National Dam Safety Program.

The members of all of the Task Groups responsible for the update of the guidelines are to be commended for their diligent and highly professional efforts.

Harold W. Andress, Jr.
Chairman, Interagency Committee on Dam Safety

EMERGENCY ACTION PLANNING FOR DAM OWNERS
TASK GROUP

Jerrold Gotzmer**
Federal Energy Regulatory Commission

Harold (Bud) W. Andress, Jr.*
Federal Emergency Management Agency

William S. Bivins*
Federal Emergency Management Agency

Ronald E. Spath*
Federal Energy Regulatory Commission

Mervin Ice
USDA, Natural Resources Conservation Service

Janet Herrin
Tennessee Valley Authority

Charles Sullivan
U.S. Army Corps of Engineers

Jan Herny
DOI, Bureau of Reclamation

**Chair of Task Group that completed final document
 *Members of Task Group that completed final document

TABLE OF CONTENTS

TABLE OF CONTENTS (Continued)

I. BASIC CONSIDERATIONS FOR PREPARING EMERGENCY ACTION PLANS

A. Purpose

1. General. There are many types of emergency events that could affect dams. Whenever people live in areas that could be flooded as a result of failure of or operation at a dam, there is a potential for loss of life and damage to property. The general purpose of these guidelines is to encourage thorough and consistent emergency action planning to help save lives and reduce property damage in areas that would be affected by dam failure or operation.

An **Emergency Action Plan (EAP)** is a formal document that identifies potential emergency conditions at a dam and specifies preplanned actions to be followed to minimize property damage and loss of life. The EAP specifies actions the dam owner [1] should take to moderate or alleviate the problems at the dam. It contains procedures and information to assist the dam owner in issuing early warning and notification messages to responsible downstream emergency management authorities of the emergency situation. It also contains inundation maps to show the emergency management authorities of the critical areas for action in case of an emergency.

2. Emergency Potential. Whenever people live in an area that could be flooded by the operation or failure of a dam, an emergency potential is assumed to exist. An **emergency** in terms of dam operation is defined as an impending or actual sudden release of water caused by an accident to, or failure of, a dam or other water retaining structure, or the result of an impending flood condition when the dam is not in danger of failure. The release of water may endanger human life or downstream property.

3. Responsibility of the Federal Emergency Management Agency. The Federal Emergency Management Agency (FEMA) is responsible for coordinating federal response to disasters and providing federal guidance to state and local emergency management authorities for all foreseeable emergencies in the United States. A recent survey indicates there are over 22,000 high or significant hazard potential dams in the United States, of which approximately 18,300, or 83 percent, do not have an EAP. The absence of an EAP at most state-regulated dams is recognized by FEMA as a deficiency in national emergency preparedness. To improve the Nation's emergency preparedness posture to respond to emergencies affecting dams, FEMA believes formal guidelines are needed to help dam owners effectively develop and exercise EAPs for dams. This process includes coordination, planning, and joint exercises involving both

---

[1] The term dam owner, as used in these guidelines, refers to the individual dam owner or the operating organization.

the EAPs of the dam owner and warning and evacuation plans of local emergency management authorities.

4. Uniformity of Plans. The effectiveness of EAPs can be enhanced by promoting a uniform format which ensures that all aspects of emergency planning are covered in each plan. Uniform EAPs and advance coordination with local and state emergency management officials and organizations should facilitate a timely response to a developing or actual emergency situation.

Organizations and individuals who own or are responsible for the operation and maintenance of dams are encouraged to use these guidelines to develop, update, and/or revise their EAPs. These guidelines supersede the *Emergency Action Planning Guidelines for Dams, FEMA 64/February 1985* and incorporate many technologically advanced emergency action planning concepts available from a wide variety of sources.

B. Scope
This document contains guidelines for preparing or revising EAPs for all high and significant hazard potential dams, *i.e.,* those dams which, if they were to fail, would be likely to cause loss of life or significant property damage. Ownership and development of the floodplain downstream from dams varies; therefore, the potential for loss of life as a result of failure or operation of a dam will also vary. **Every EAP must be tailored to site-specific conditions.**

EAPs generally contain six basic elements:

- Notification Flowchart
- Emergency Detection, Evaluation, and Classification
- Responsibilities
- Preparedness
- Inundation Maps
- Appendices

All of the elements should be included in a complete EAP. The dam owner is responsible for the development of the EAP. However, the development or revision of an EAP must be done in coordination with those having emergency management responsibilities at the state and local levels. Emergency management agencies will use the information in a dam owner's EAP to facilitate the implementation of their responsibilities. State and local emergency management authorities will generally have some type of plan in place, either a Local Emergency Operations Plan or a Warning and Evacuation Plan.

C. The Six Basic Elements of an EAP This section lists and briefly examines why there is a need for the six basic elements of an EAP. The requirements of these elements are discussed in detail in Chapter II of these guidelines, which presents a recommended format for uniformity among EAPs.

1. Notification Flowchart. A notification flowchart shows who is to be notified, by whom, and in what priority. The information on the notification flowchart is necessary for the timely notification of persons responsible for taking emergency actions.

2. Emergency Detection, Evaluation, and Classification. Early detection and evaluation of the situation(s) or triggering event(s) that initiate or require an emergency action are crucial. The establishment of procedures for reliable and **timely** classification of an emergency situation is imperative to ensure that the appropriate course of action is taken based on the urgency of the situation. It is better to activate the EAP while confirming the extent of the emergency than to wait for the emergency to occur.

3. Responsibilities. A determination of responsibility for EAP-related tasks must be made during the development of the plan. Dam owners are responsible for developing, maintaining, and implementing the EAP. State and local emergency management officials having statutory obligation are responsible for warning and evacuation within affected areas. The EAP must clearly specify the dam owner's responsibilities to ensure effective, timely action is taken should an emergency occur at the dam. The EAP must be site-specific because conditions at the dam and downstream of all dams are different.

4. Preparedness. Preparedness actions are taken to moderate or alleviate the effects of a dam failure or operational spillway release and to facilitate response to emergencies. This section identifies actions to be taken before any emergency.

5. Inundation Maps. An inundation map should delineate the areas that would be flooded as a result of a dam failure. Inundation maps are used both by the dam owner and emergency management officials to facilitate timely notification and evacuation of areas affected by a dam failure or flood condition. These maps greatly facilitate notification by graphically displaying flooded areas and showing travel times for wave front and flood peaks at critical locations.

6. Appendices. The appendices contain information that supports and supplements the material used in the development and maintenance of the EAP.

D. Coordination
It is vital that development of the EAP be coordinated with all entities, jurisdictions, and agencies that would be affected by a dam failure and/or flooding as a result of large operational releases, or that have statutory responsibilities for warning, evacuation, and post-flood actions. The finished product should be user friendly as it realistically takes into account each organization's capabilities and responsibilities.

Coordination with state and local emergency management officials at appropriate levels of management responsible for warning and evacuation of the public is essential to ensure that there is agreement on their individual and group responsibilities. Participation in the preparation of the EAP will enhance their confidence in the EAP and in the accuracy of its components. Coordination will provide opportunities for discussion and determination of the order in which public officials would be notified, backup personnel, alternate means of communication, and special procedures for nighttime, holidays, and weekends.

The tasks and responsibilities of the dam owner and the emergency management officials that would be implemented during a dam emergency incident need to be as compatible as possible.

To facilitate compatibility, the dam owner should coordinate emergency response actions with the local emergency management officials who have the responsibility to provide a timely warning and evacuation notice to populations at risk. This should help prevent over, or under, reaction to the incident by various organizations.

E. Evacuation
Evacuation planning and implementation are the responsibility of the state and local officials who are responsible for the safety of the public who live in areas that would be inundated by failure of a dam or flood releases. The dam owner should not usurp the responsibility of the local authorities responsible for evacuation. However, there may be situations where recreational facilities, campgrounds, or residences may be located below a dam where local authorities would not be able to issue a timely warning. In such cases, the dam owner should coordinate with local emergency management officials to determine who will warn these people and in what priority.

F. Emergency Duration, Security, Termination, and Follow-up
An EAP needs to address who in the dam owner's organization will issue status reports during the emergency, when and how a declared emergency will be terminated, what security provisions shall be maintained at the dam, and plans for a follow-up evaluation and report.

1. Emergency Duration. Emergency situations that occur at a dam will require that status reports and situation assessments be provided by the dam owner to appropriate organizations throughout the duration of the incident.

2. Security Provisions. An EAP should consider security provisions at and surrounding the dam during emergency conditions to protect the public and permit effective performance of emergency response actions.

3. Emergency Termination. There are two conditions requiring a termination of the emergency. One has to do with emergency conditions at the dam and the other is related to the evacuation and disaster response. The dam owner is usually responsible for making the decision that an emergency condition no longer exists at the dam. The EAP should clearly designate the responsible party. The applicable state or local emergency management officials are responsible for termination of the evacuation or disaster response activities.

The dam owner and state and local officials should agree on when it is appropriate to terminate an emergency. The dam owner should cooperate with state and local officials to determine if a news release which can be used by the media for broadcast to the general public notifying them of termination of the emergency condition is appropriate. Such news releases are expected to be a supplement to other methods of notifying the public that the emergency has been terminated.

4. Follow-up Evaluation. Following an emergency, an evaluation and review should be conducted that includes all participants. The following should be discussed and evaluated in the after-action review:

- Events before, during, and following the emergency

- Significant actions taken by each participant, and improvements practicable for future emergencies

- All strengths and deficiencies found in procedures, materials, equipment, staffing levels, and leadership

The results of the after-action review should be documented in an evaluation report chaired by the dam owner and used as a basis for revising the EAP.

G. Maintaining an EAP

After the EAP has been developed, approved, and distributed, the job is not done. Without periodic maintenance, the EAP will become out-dated, lose its effectiveness, and no longer be workable. If the plan is not exercised (verified), those involved in its implementation may become unfamiliar with their roles and responsibilities, particularly if emergency response personnel change. If the plan is not updated, the information contained in it may become outdated and useless.

1. Exercising. Emergency incidents at dams and/or dam failures are not common events. Therefore, training and exercises are necessary to maintain operational readiness, timeliness, and responsiveness. The status of training and levels of readiness should be evaluated in non-threatening simulated periodic emergency exercises for key personnel of the dam owner.

Key personnel from state and local emergency management agencies should be encouraged to participate in any training and exercises of the EAP whenever possible and as appropriate.

The dam owner should exercise the EAP because it promotes emergency preparedness, mitigation, and response, and demonstrates how effective the EAP will be in an actual emergency situation. Periodic exercises will result in an improved EAP as lessons learned during the exercise can be incorporated into an updated EAP document.

There are five types of exercises in an exercise program. It is not a requirement that every exercise program include all five exercises. However, it is advisable to build an exercise program upon competencies developed from simpler exercises to achieve greater success with the more complex exercises. This means that emergency exercises should be developed and conducted in an ascending order of complexity. **It is important that sufficient time be provided between each exercise to learn and improve from the experiences of the previous exercise before conducting a more complex exercise.** The five exercise types, listed from simplest to most complex, are described below.

a. Orientation Seminar - This exercise is a seminar that involves bringing together those with a role or interest in an EAP, *i.e.*, dam owner and state and local emergency management agencies, to discuss the EAP and initial plans for an annual drill or more in-depth comprehensive exercise. The seminar does not involve an actual exercise of the EAP. Instead, it is a meeting that enables each participant to become familiar with the EAP and the roles, responsibilities, and procedures of those involved. An orientation seminar can also be used to discuss and describe technical matters with involved, non-technical personnel.

b. Drill - A drill is the lowest level exercise that involves an actual exercise. It tests, develops, or maintains skills in a single emergency response procedure. An example of a drill is an in-house exercise performed to verify the validity of telephone numbers and other means of communication along with the dam owner's response. A drill is considered a necessary part of ongoing training.

c. Tabletop Exercise - The tabletop exercise is a higher level exercise than the drill. The tabletop exercise involves a meeting of the dam owner and the state and local emergency management officials in a conference room environment. The format is usually informal with minimum stress involved. The exercise begins with the description of a simulated event and proceeds with discussions by the participants to evaluate the EAP and response procedures and to resolve concerns regarding coordination and responsibilities.

d. Functional Exercise - The functional exercise is the highest level exercise that does not involve the full activation of the dam owner and state and local emergency management agency field personnel and facilities or test evacuation of residents downstream of the dam. It involves the various levels of the dam owner and state and local emergency management personnel that would be involved in an actual emergency. The functional exercise takes place in a stress-induced environment with time constraints and involves the simulation of a dam failure and other specified events. The participants "act out" their actual roles. The exercise is designed to evaluate both the internal capabilities and responses of the dam owner and the workability of the information in the EAP used by the emergency management officials to carry out their responsibilities. The functional exercise also is designed to evaluate the coordination activities between the dam owner and emergency management personnel.

e. Full Scale Exercise - The full scale exercise is the most complex level of exercise. It evaluates the operational capability of all facets of the emergency management system (both dam owner and state and local emergency management agencies) interactively in a stressful environment with the actual mobilization of personnel and resources. It includes field movement and deployment to demonstrate coordination and response capability. The participants actively "play out" their roles in a dynamic environment that provides the highest degree of realism possible for the simulated event. Actual evacuation of critical residents may be exercised if previously announced to the public.

A comprehensive EAP exercise is an in-depth EAP exercise that simulates a dam failure and involves the active interaction and participation of the dam owner with state and local emergency management personnel in a stressful environment with time constraints. Functional and full scale exercises are considered comprehensive exercises. The basic difference between these two exercise types is that a full scale exercise involves actual field movement and mobilization, whereas field activity is simulated in a functional exercise. A comprehensive exercise provides the necessary verification, training, and practice to improve the EAP and the operational readiness and coordination efforts of all parties responsible for responding to emergencies at a dam, such as failure, misoperation, and sabotage.

For most dam owners, the orientation seminar, drill, tabletop exercise, and functional exercise should receive the most emphasis in their EAP exercise programs. It is recommended that dam owners conduct a functional exercises at least once every 5 years. Tabletop exercises are usually conducted on a more frequent basis.

Full scale exercises should be considered as optional emergency exercise activities, and should be conducted primarily when there is a specific need to evaluate actual field movement and deployment. When a full scale exercise is conducted, safety becomes a major concern because of the extensive field activity. If a dam owner has the capability to conduct a full scale exercise, a commitment should be made to schedule and conduct the entire series of exercises listed above before conducting any full scale exercise. This will also require that at least one functional exercise be conducted before conducting a full scale exercise. Functional and full scale exercises can be coordinated with other scheduled exercises to share emergency management agency resources and reduce costs.

The primary objectives of a comprehensive exercise are to:

(1) Reveal the strengths and weaknesses of the EAP, including specified internal actions, external notification procedures, and adequacy of other information, such as inundation maps.

(2) Reveal deficiencies in resources and information available to the dam owner and the state and local agencies.

(3) Improve coordination efforts between the dam owner and the state and local agencies. Close coordination and cooperation among all responsible parties is vital for a successful response to an actual emergency.

(4) Clarify the roles and responsibilities of the dam owner and the state and local emergency management officials.

(5) Improve individual performance of the people who respond to the dam failure or other emergency conditions.

(6) Gain public recognition of the EAP.

Testing of monitoring, sensing, and warning equipment at remote/unattended dams should be included in emergency exercise activities.

Emergency exercises and equipment tests should be evaluated orally and in writing, and the EAP should be revised and corrected, as necessary. Immediately following an exercise or actual emergency, an evaluation of the EAP should be conducted with all involved parties. The evaluation should focus on the procedures and other information in the EAP, not on the performance of the individuals who carried out the established procedures. It should address both the procedures that worked well and the procedures that did not work so well. The responses from all participants involved in the exercise should be considered. The exercise evaluation should discuss and evaluate the events before, during, and following the exercise or actual emergency; actions taken by each participant; the **time** required to become aware of an emergency and to implement the EAP; and the improvements practicable for future emergencies.

The purpose of the evaluation is to identify strengths and deficiencies in the EAP, such as outdated telephone numbers on the notification chart, inundation maps with inaccurate information, and problems with procedures, priorities, assigned responsibilities, materials, equipment, and staff levels. After the evaluation has been completed, the EAP should be revised, as appropriate, and the revisions disseminated to all involved parties.

2. Updating. In addition to regular exercises, a periodic (at least annual) review of the overall EAP should be conducted to assess its workability and efficiency, *i.e.*, timeliness of implementation, and to improve weak areas.

Changes that may frequently require revision and update of an EAP include changes in personnel of various organizations and changes in communications systems. Therefore, a periodic review of telephone numbers and appropriate personnel included in the notification flowchart should be conducted.

A review should be made of any changes to the dam and/or floodplain as this may affect the information on the inundation maps. Changes to the maps should be made as soon as practical and noted in the EAP.

Once the plan has been revised, the updated version--or simply the affected pages-- should be distributed to all involved parties. The distribution of copies of the EAP and the notification flowchart (if issued separately) must be controlled and documented to ensure simultaneous updating of **all** copies. Updates should be made promptly. In addition, it is recommended that the entire EAP be reprinted and distributed to all parties at least every 5 years.

II. SUGGESTED EAP FORMAT

A. The Format

A suggested format is provided in these guidelines to ensure all six basic elements are included in an EAP, to provide uniformity, and to encourage thorough and consistent emergency action planning for levels of preparedness that may save lives and reduce property damage in areas affected by dam operation or failure. It is important that dam owner and regulatory requirements be satisfied when selecting a format for an EAP.

Although it is not necessary to follow exactly the format outlined below, it is necessary that all EAPs within a given jurisdiction be similar and consistent to eliminate confusion when activating any EAP. To the extent possible, an EAP should be organized in the format that is most useful for those involved in the plan. The EAP must be user friendly so that it will actually be used during EAP exercises and actual emergency events. Regardless of the format used, development of an EAP should consider the elements described on the following pages to ensure all aspects of emergency action planning are covered.

It is helpful to place the EAP in a loose-leaf binder so that outdated pages (or the entire EAP) can be easily removed and replaced with updated information, and to ensure a complete, current, and workable plan. It is also beneficial to place the date of the EAP or current revisions on each page.

The suggested format for an EAP appears below.

SUGGESTED EAP FORMAT

Title Page/Cover Sheet

Table of Contents

I.   Notification Flowchart
II. Statement of Purpose
III. Project Description
IV. Emergency Detection, Evaluation, and Classification
V.   General Responsibilities Under the EAP
    A.   Dam Owner Responsibilities
    B.   Responsibility for Notification
    C.   Responsibility for Evacuation
    D.   Responsibility for Termination and Follow-Up
    E.   EAP Coordinator Responsibility
VI. Preparedness
VII. Inundation Maps

VIII. Appendices
   A.   Investigation and Analyses of Dambreak Floods
   B.   Plans for Training, Exercising, Updating, and Posting the EAP
   C.   Site-Specific Concerns
   D.   Approval of the EAP

The suggested format was purposefully devised to separate an EAP into two distinct sections: the basic EAP and the Appendices which, when combined together, constitute a complete EAP.

1. The Basic EAP. Sections I through VII of the format constitute the basic EAP, *i.e.*, they contain information that will likely be used by **all** parties (both the dam owner and emergency management officials) during an actual emergency. For example, the dam owner will use the notification flowchart to issue its emergency warning to the appropriate officials in a prioritized order. Similarly, the emergency management officials will use the flowchart to contact other officials or the dam owner, as needed, throughout the emergency. As a second example, both the dam owner and the emergency management officials will use the inundation maps extensively in fulfilling their responsibilities.

It must be remembered that the responsibilities of the state and local emergency management authorities and other organizations in the jurisdictions affected by a dam failure or flooding as a result of operation of a dam are not included in an EAP. Information unique to state and local emergency management authorities, and any other organizations that would have responsibilities for the warning and evacuation of populations at risk, would be included in the portion(s) of the appropriate jurisdiction's Emergency Operations Plan dedicated specifically to warning and evacuation of populations placed at risk as a result of dam failure or flooding due to large operational releases. However, the information in the EAP must be coordinated with the appropriate authorities because they will depend on and use the information in the dam owner's EAP to help them carry out their responsibilities.

2. The Appendices. The Appendices are an important element which completes the EAP. However, the information contained in the Appendices is not necessarily needed by all parties during an actual emergency. They typically contain support materials used in the development of the basic EAP. More specifically, the Appendices focus on important issues such as those that specifically address maintenance requirements for the EAP and dambreak investigations and analyses, among others. This information may be directly applicable to the actions of the dam owner and possibly some of the emergency management parties, but may not be critical to the actions and activities of other parties during an actual emergency.

All emergency management officials should be offered the complete EAP. However, it may be left to their discretion to decide whether they want to receive a copy of the complete EAP (basic EAP + Appendices) or the basic EAP. **Those who elect to receive the basic EAP should understand that if it does not provide sufficient information for them to perform their functions, they should obtain the complete EAP.**

NOTE: *Every EAP must be tailored to site-specific conditions and to the requirements of the organization that owns, operates, or regulates the use of the dam. This can be accomplished under the suggested format. Uniformity of EAPs is important because any one state or local emergency management agency may be affected by a river system that has a series of dams, the independent failure or operation of which may impact the jurisdiction. Uniformity provides for clarity and better understanding of the information in the EAP for each individual dam.*

B. Format Items Defined
This section follows the heading and numbering of the suggested format and describes in detail each element of an EAP.

Title Page/Cover Sheet
An EAP document's cover identifies it as an Emergency Action Plan and specifies the dam for which it was developed. Since each dam must have its own EAP with its own specific procedures to be followed, title pages or cover sheets are essential so that personnel can be sure that they are using the right EAP for the circumstances. To assist state and federal dam safety personnel, include the National Inventory of Dams number unique to each dam on the title page.

Table of Contents
List all major items in the Table of Contents, including flow charts, figures, and tables.

I. Notification Flowchart
The EAP should begin with one notification flowchart that clearly summarizes the following information and is applicable to each of the emergency classification levels considered (see discussion under Section IV).

- Who is responsible for notifying each dam owner representative(s) and/or emergency management official(s)

- What is the prioritized order in which individuals are to be notified

- Who is to be notified

The notification flowchart should include individual names and position titles, office and home telephone numbers, alternative contacts, and means of communication, *e.g.*, radio call numbers. The number of persons to be notified by each responsible individual on the notification flowchart should be governed by what other responsibilities the person has been assigned. It is usually recommended that any one individual not be responsible for contacting more than three or four other parties.

The notification list should consider the following individuals and organizations.

- Dam owner
- Local emergency management officials and other organizations
- Appropriate federal and state emergency management agencies
- Residents and property owners located immediately downstream of the dam within the boundary of potential inundation where available warning time is very limited
- Operators of other dams or water-retention facilities
- Managers and operators of recreation facilities
- National Weather Service
- News media[2]
- Others, as appropriate

Although the list above is not all inclusive or prioritized, both the dam owner and the local, state, and federal emergency management authorities are typically given top priority in the notification flowchart.

The notification flowchart should be easy to follow for each emergency classification level (see Section IV). One flowchart that represents all levels is preferred for the sake of effectiveness and simplicity. However, for clarity it might be necessary to develop a flowchart for each classification level. Color coding, *i.e.*, using different colored lines to trace the proper sequence of notification under various emergency classification levels, may prove helpful. If necessary, narrative information supplementing the flowchart may be provided on the page following the flowchart.

NOTE: *Information is exchanged both up and down the notification flowchart.*

---

[2] The news media, including radio, television, and newspapers, should be utilized to the extent available and appropriate. Use of news media should be preplanned to the extent possible by the dam owner or emergency management officials. Notification to the news media may be by the dam owner or emergency management officials depending on the type of emergency. Notification plans should define emergency situations for which each medium will be utilized and should include an example of a news release that would be the most effective for each possible emergency. Information for the media ordinarily should not be relied upon as the primary means of warning.

Copies of the flowchart should be readily available to each individual having responsibilities under the plan, and should be kept up-to-date through exercises and revisions.

NOTE: *The flowchart on the next page is only a sample flowchart. A flowchart must be tailored to the specific needs and notification priorities of the dam to which it applies.*

SAMPLE NOTIFICATION FLOWCHART

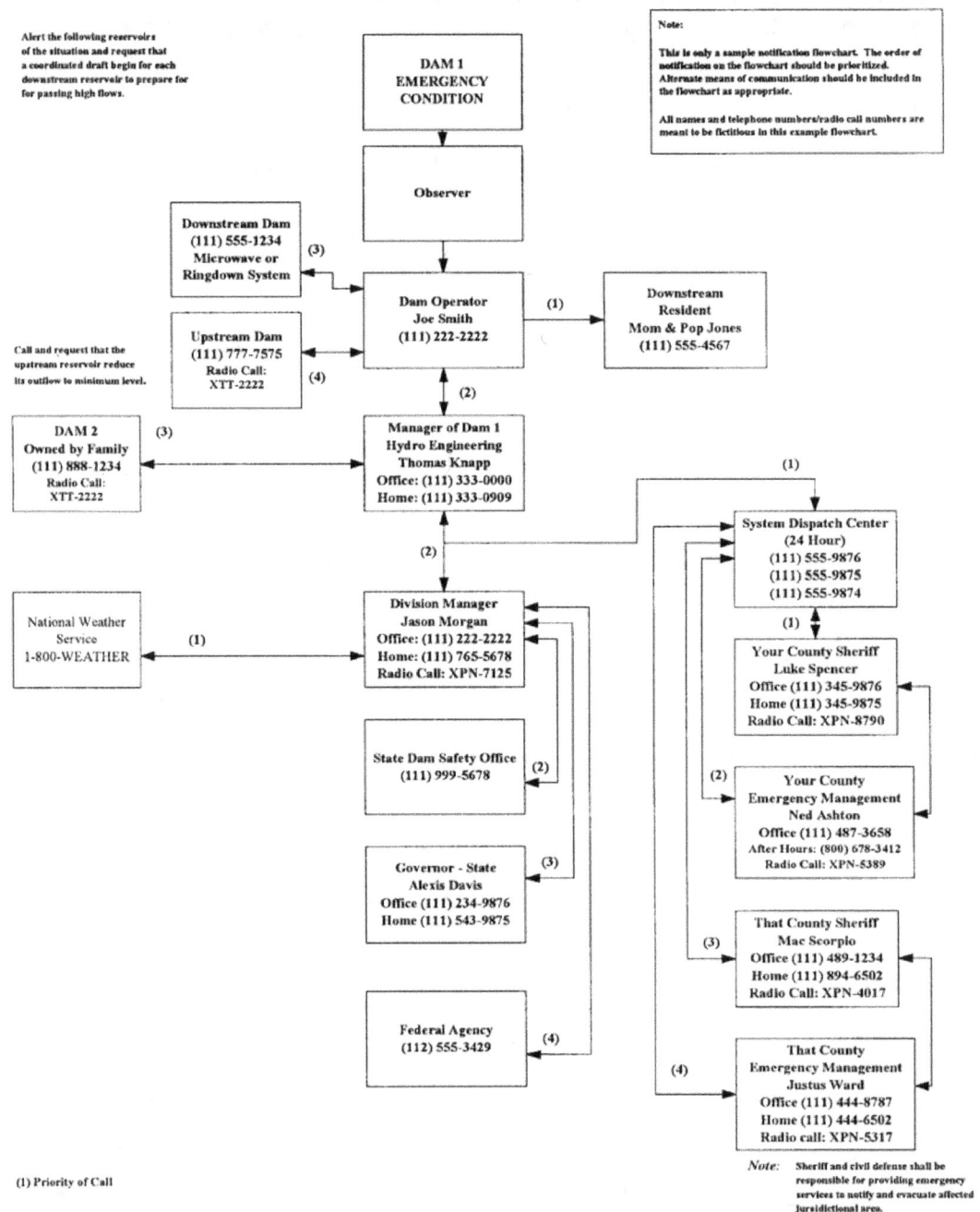

Alert the following reservoirs of the situation and request that a coordinated draft begin for each downstream reservoir to prepare for for passing high flows.

Note:

This is only a sample notification flowchart. The order of notification on the flowchart should be prioritized. Alternate means of communication should be included in the flowchart as appropriate.

All names and telephone numbers/radio call numbers are meant to be fictitious in this example flowchart.

DAM 1 EMERGENCY CONDITION

Observer

Downstream Dam (111) 555-1234 Microwave or Ringdown System (3)

Dam Operator Joe Smith (111) 222-2222 (1)

Downstream Resident Mom & Pop Jones (111) 555-4567

Upstream Dam (111) 777-7575 Radio Call: XTT-2222 (4)

Call and request that the upstream reservoir reduce its outflow to minimum level.

(2)

DAM 2 Owned by Family (111) 888-1234 Radio Call: XTT-2222 (3)

Manager of Dam 1 Hydro Engineering Thomas Knapp Office: (111) 333-0000 Home: (111) 333-0909

(1)

System Dispatch Center (24 Hour) (111) 555-9876 (111) 555-9875 (111) 555-9874

(2)

(1)

National Weather Service 1-800-WEATHER (1)

Division Manager Jason Morgan Office: (111) 222-2222 Home: (111) 765-5678 Radio Call: XPN-7125

Your County Sheriff Luke Spencer Office (111) 345-9876 Home (111) 345-9875 Radio Call: XPN-8790

(1)

(2) **Your County Emergency Management** Ned Ashton Office (111) 487-3658 After Hours: (800) 678-3412 Radio Call: XPN-5389

State Dam Safety Office (111) 999-5678 (2)

Governor - State Alexis Davis Office (111) 234-9876 Home (111) 543-9875 (3)

(3) **That County Sheriff** Mac Scorpio Office (111) 489-1234 Home (111) 894-6502 Radio Call: XPN-4017

Federal Agency (112) 555-3429 (4)

(4) **That County Emergency Management** Justus Ward Office (111) 444-8787 Home (111) 444-6502 Radio call: XPN-5317

(1) Priority of Call

Note: Sheriff and civil defense shall be responsible for providing emergency services to notify and evacuate affected jurisdictional area.

II. Statement of Purpose

Following the notification flowchart, briefly state the purpose and scope of the EAP. Two examples of a statement of purpose are shown below.

Example 1: "This plan defines responsibilities and provides procedures designed to identify unusual and unlikely conditions which may endanger Any Dam in time to take mitigative action and to notify the appropriate emergency management officials of possible, impending, or actual failure of the dam. The plan may also be used to provide notification when flood releases will create major flooding."

Example 2: "The purpose of this Emergency Action Plan (EAP) is to safeguard the lives and reduce damage to the property of the citizens of Alpha County living along Beta Creek, in the event of failure of the Beta Creek Dam or flooding caused by large runoff."

III. Project Description

Provide a description of the project and its location. Include a project vicinity map and a simple drawing showing project features. List any significant upstream or downstream dams. List downstream communities potentially affected by a dam failure or by flooding as a result of large operational releases.

IV. Emergency Detection, Evaluation, and Classification

The EAP document should include a discussion of procedures for timely and reliable detection, evaluation, and classification of an existing or potential emergency condition.

The conditions, events, or measures for **detection** of an existing or potential emergency should be listed. Data and information collection systems (early warning system hardware, rule curves, or other information related to abnormal reservoir levels, inspection/monitoring plan, inspection procedures, instrumentation plan) should be discussed. The process that will be used to analyze incoming data should also be described.

Procedures, aids, instruction, and provisions for **evaluation** of information and data to assess the severity and magnitude of any existing or potential emergency should be discussed.

Emergencies are classified according to their severity and urgency. An emergency **classification** system is one means to classify emergency events according to the different times at which they occur and to their varying levels of severity. The classification system indicates the urgency of the emergency condition. **Emergency classifications should use terms agreed to by the dam owner and emergency management officials during the planning process, in order for the system to**

work and to ensure organizations understand terminology and respond appropriately to the event.

Titles for emergency classifications should be chosen carefully by the organizations that will use them so that everyone will understand what each classification level means when notifications are issued and received.

Declaration of an emergency can be a very controversial decision. The issue should not be debated too long. An early decision and declaration are critical to maximize available response time.

Some locations may require only two emergency classifications, while others may require more. For the purpose of these EAP guidelines, **two dam failure emergency classifications** and one **non-failure emergency classification** are provided:

- Failure is imminent or has occurred (Condition A)
- Potential failure situation is developing (Condition B)
- Non-failure emergency condition

The definition of these conditions follows.

Failure is imminent or has occurred (Condition A)
Generally, this situation should convey the impression that "time has run out" with respect to the failure of the dam. This is a situation where a failure either has occurred, is occurring, or obviously is just about to occur. The question is often asked, "how much time is available when failure is considered to be imminent?" It is impossible to determine how long it will take for a failure to occur or for a complete breach to occur once failure begins. **Therefore, once a dam owner determines that there is no longer any time available to attempt corrective measures to prevent failure, the "failure is imminent or has occurred" warning should be issued.** Emergency management agencies, for evacuation purposes, should conservatively interpret the phrase "failure is imminent" to mean that the dam is failing, *i.e.,* it should not be assumed that there is some time lag between "failure is imminent" and a "failure has occurred." Therefore, "failure is imminent" and "failure has occurred" should conservatively be interpreted as essentially the same condition for evacuation purposes.

Potential failure situation is developing (Condition B)
Generally, this situation should convey the impression that "some amount of time" is still available for further analyses/decisions to be made before dam failure is considered to be a foregone conclusion. This a situation where a failure may eventually occur but pre-planned actions taken during certain events (such as major floods, earthquakes, evidence of piping) may moderate or alleviate failure. Even if failure is inevitable, more

time is generally available than in a failure has occurred situation to issue warnings and/or take preparedness actions.

Is the time frame for this situation in hours, days, or weeks? When a dam safety situation is observed that may lead to a failure if left unattended but there is no immediate danger, the dam owner should issue a warning that a "potential failure situation is developing." The dam owner should assess the situation and determine the urgency of the emergency situation. Based on the dam owner's assessment (and as a result of prior coordination with the appropriate authorities), the authorities should be placed on alert and it is up to the authorities to determine the appropriate course of action.

If it appears that a situation may take days or weeks before it could develop into a failure situation, the local authorities may decide on one course of action. Periodic status report updates from the dam owner are important because when it appears that the situation is continuing to worsen at the dam, in spite of the actions being taken to moderate or alleviate failure, the local authorities may decide to change their course of action. Depending on the location of downstream residents with respect to the dam and the estimated warning time available, the evacuating agencies should consider the prudence of early evacuation, or heightened awareness, of certain downstream areas until the emergency has passed.

NOTE: *It should be remembered that it may be appropriate to immediately declare a Condition A. However, there should be smooth transition from Condition B to Condition A when using Condition B initially.*

To assist the evacuating agencies in selecting their appropriate course of action and to provide a proper transition from Condition B to Condition A, dam owners should clearly communicate their assessment of the situation to the agencies. The dam owner should consider placing the agencies on an initial alert and provide periodic updates on the situation as it develops so that the agencies can assess when they should implement their evacuation procedures. For example, a dam owner could issue an initial warning and periodic updates on the reservoir level as it rises during flood conditions and eventually overtops an embankment dam. As the reservoir rises, "a potential failure situation is developing" warning should be implemented with periodic updates on how much time is available before the embankment overtops. Immediately before the embankment overtops, a "failure is imminent or has occurred" warning should be issued.

Non-failure emergency condition
Generally, this situation should be used when there is no danger of dam failure, but flow conditions are such that flooding is expected to occur downstream of the dam. Non-failure emergency conditions are more common than the failure emergency conditions.

Activation of the EAP will provide an early warning to downstream areas during flood conditions or large spillway releases. Therefore, an important application of the EAP is when there is a flood occurring on the river system, but there may be no apparent threat to the integrity of the dam. In this situation, natural flooding is expected or is in progress upstream from the dam site and an impending or actual release of water to downstream areas will result from unusually large spillway releases or passage of unusually large flows at dams having uncontrolled spillways. The dam owner can provide an important public service by notifying the appropriate agencies of the expected release or passage of flood waters below the dam. While the amount of flooding may be beyond the control the dam owner, information on the amount of releases from the dam will be very helpful to the authorities in reaching any decisions on the need for evacuation.

V. General Responsibilities Under the Plan

The plan should specify the person(s) or organization responsible for the maintenance and operation of the dam and the persons or groups responsible for implementing various phases of the EAP. Some specific responsibilities to be considered are discussed below.

A. Dam Owner Responsibilities

The duties of the dam owner or owner's designated representatives under the EAP should be clearly described. Some suggestions for information to include in this section follow.

The operators should be advised of the importance of the EAP and why the EAP is necessary. The operators' duties under the EAP should be described. Include pointers on how to communicate the emergency situation to those who need to be contacted along with samples of typical communications.

Specific actions operators are to take **after** implementing the EAP notification procedures should be described. For example, opening spillway gates, especially if a certain sequence is desired, and opening/closing water intakes, as appropriate. Instructions for the operation of the project during the anticipated emergency should be provided.

The chain of command should be described. Officials and alternates of the dam owner who must be notified should be designated and priority of notification determined. Notification of supervisory personnel on the dam owner's staff is desirable, if time permits. Advice may be needed concerning predetermined remedial action to delay, moderate, or alleviate the severity of the emergency condition. The responsibilities required by the EAP should be coordinated with appropriate levels of management to ensure full awareness of organizational capabilities and responsibilities. EAPs must always be developed as a result of coordination and consultation with other entities and agencies that will be affected by a failure of a dam, or large operational releases, or have statutory responsibilities in warning and evacuation.

B. Responsibility for Notification

The person(s) authorized to notify state and local officials should be determined and **clearly identified** in the EAP. If time allows in an emergency situation, onsite personnel should seek advice and assistance. However, under certain circumstances, such as when failure is imminent or has occurred, the responsibility and authority for notification may have to be delegated to the dam operator or a local official. Such situations should be specified in the EAP.

The accurate and timely dissemination of emergency public information is very important to the overall success of an EAP. The person who is responsible for disseminating information to the media and the public on a periodic basis throughout the emergency should be designated. If resources are available, an exclusive public information officer should be identified to disseminate all media briefs. The means for keeping local authorities advised of continuing conditions at the dam also should be described.

Dam owners should develop procedures for dissemination of **dam specific** information to the media in anticipation of questions the media may have about the incident as it applies to the dam. A procedure like this should, in effect, help minimize the potential for dissemination of misinformation and spreading of false rumors.

Throughout the United States, the National Weather Service (NWS) and/or other agencies have the general responsibility for issuing flood warnings. It may be beneficial to include the appropriate agency having this responsibility on the notification chart so that its facilities can enhance warnings being issued.

Local agencies will usually establish an Emergency Operations Center (EOC), or Incident Command System (ICS), to serve as the main distribution center for warning and evacuation activities. The availability of specific local resources should be determined through discussion and orientation seminars with local agency personnel. Proper coordination and communication among onsite technical personnel at the dam, public information officer(s), and emergency personnel at the EOC is of critical importance to a successful EAP. Thorough verification during comprehensive EAP exercises will greatly assist in providing this smooth interface.

C. Responsibility for Evacuation

Warning and evacuation planning are the responsibilities of local authorities who have the statutory obligation. Under the EAP, the dam owner is responsible for notifying the appropriate emergency management officials when flooding is anticipated, or a failure is imminent or has occurred.

Dam owners should not assume, or usurp, the responsibility of government entities for evacuation of people. However, there may be situations in which routine notification and evacuation will not suffice, as in the case of a resident located just downstream of the dam. In this case, the dam owner should arrange to notify that person directly. **This procedure should be coordinated with the appropriate public officials before an emergency situation develops.**

D. Responsibility for Duration, Security, Termination, and Follow-Up
A person should be designated for on-site monitoring of the situation at the dam and keeping local authorities informed of developing conditions at the dam from the time that an emergency starts until the emergency has been terminated.

Provisions for security measures at the dam during the emergency should be specified.

A person should also be responsible for declaring that the emergency at the dam is terminated. The applicable state or local emergency management officials are responsible for termination of the disaster response activities.

A follow-up evaluation after an emergency by all participants should be specified. The results of the evaluation should be documented in a written report.

E. EAP Coordinator Responsibility
The dam owner should specify in the EAP the designated EAP coordinator who will be responsible for EAP-related activities, including (but not limited to) preparing revisions to the EAP, establishing training seminars, and coordinating EAP exercises. This person should be the EAP contact if any involved parties have questions about the plan.

VI. Preparedness
Preparedness actions are taken to prevent a dam failure incident or to help reduce the effects of a dam failure or operational spillway release and facilitate response to emergencies. A few of the preparedness actions that a dam owner may take include providing emergency flood operating instructions and arranging for equipment, labor, and materials for use in emergency situations.

The EAP should describe preparedness actions taken both before and following the development of emergency conditions. Preparedness actions involve the installation of equipment or the establishment of procedures for one or more of the following purposes.

> Preventing emergency conditions from developing, if possible, or warning of the development of emergency situations.

- Facilitating the operation of the dam to limit impacts in an emergency situation.

- Minimizing the extent of damage resulting from any emergency situations that do develop.

The need for **timely** action in an emergency situation cannot be overemphasized. The EAP should contain a discussion of provisions for surveillance and evaluation of an emergency situation and should clearly indicate that emergency response procedures can be implemented in a timely manner. An important factor in the effectiveness of the EAP is the prompt detection and evaluation of information obtained from instrumentation and/or physical inspection procedures.

In the EAP, discuss the time factor from the actual occurrence of an emergency to awareness of the emergency, and its effect on the workability of the EAP. **Timely implementation of the EAP and coordination and communication with downstream local authorities are crucial elements in the effectiveness of emergency response to the incident.**

There are several types of preparedness actions that should be considered when developing an EAP. These actions include:

- Surveillance
- Response during periods of darkness
- Access to the site
- Response during weekends and holidays
- Response during periods of adverse weather
- Alternative systems of communication
- Emergency supplies and information

The following sections discuss each of these actions.

A. Surveillance
The EAP should contain a discussion of provisions for surveillance, detection, and evaluation of an emergency situation and should clearly indicate that the EAP can be implemented in a timely manner.

When a dam is not continuously attended and dam failure or operational releases would endanger human life or cause significant property damage, it is imperative that procedures be developed to identify conditions requiring emergency actions, and to promptly alert emergency management officials responsible for warning and evacuation of residents who would be affected in the event of an emergency at the dam. To be able to promptly notify responsible officials of emergency conditions, a dam owner should be able to detect and evaluate developing emergency conditions. The information system must be able to deliver clear, concise, and reliable data so that the responsible official(s) may react with confidence and implement the EAP. While the EAP is being activated, personnel should visit the site to verify conditions.

For an unattended dam, a remote surveillance system that includes instrumentation and telemetering facilities at the dam site should be considered to provide a continuous reading of headwater and tailwater levels. If the dam owner has an operations control center that is attended 24 hours a day, the system should include a computer at the operations center to monitor the data and to activate an audible alarm whenever the rate of change of the headwater or tailwater over a given period of time exceeds prescribed limits. The alarm also should be activated if the headwater or tailwater elevations exceed prescribed maximum or minimum levels. Design must be site-specific. The limits programmed in a system must account for changes in headwater and tailwater levels that would occur during normal dam operation, floods, and maintenance.

Monitoring of the tailwater generally is more sensitive to changes resulting from a breach of the structures than monitoring the headwater. Changes in tailwater will alert operators more quickly to site conditions and help determine whether emergency management officials should be notified. If continuous readings of both the headwater and tailwater are available, the operator can obtain a current reading at any time and check conditions at the site after an alarm is sounded.

Provisions should be made for the alarm to sound when there is an interruption of power to, and loss of communication with, the monitoring instrumentation. (When a dam tender lives close to the project, an alarm should be installed in the dam tender's house.) When power to or communication with the site is interrupted, the dam should be manned until conditions are returned to normal. Operation of the alarms should be checked periodically. Proper functioning of alarms should be confirmed by testing. For instance, annual testing of the EAP might be initiated by artificially tripping one of the alarms.

Reaction time must be minimized when inhabited structures are located immediately downstream of the dam. When these conditions exist, special procedures may need to be included in the EAP to notify the occupants involved. Local officials should be fully involved in the development of these special procedures.

The EAP should describe any instrumentation for monitoring the behavior of unattended dams, and explain how warning systems would be activated. Instrumentation responses should be instantaneous to facilitate immediate action by operators.

Procedures should be described for providing continuous surveillance for periods of actual or forecasted high flows. It may be necessary to send an observer to the dam during these periods, and not rely on the instrumentation alone. It is very important that an observer be at the dam when flood conditions or signs of serious structural distress have been identified.

If a discussion of remote surveillance at the dam is not applicable, that fact should be stated in the EAP.

B. Response During Periods of Darkness
Discussion in the EAP of the response to potential or actual emergency conditions during periods of darkness should be addressed.

Actions to be taken to illuminate the spillway operating deck, or observation of distressed areas of the dam, and other actions that will facilitate the operation of gates or other emergency equipment should be described.

Any special procedures for contacting or notifying the proper personnel, local officials, or others during a power failure should be described.

The expected response time for verifying an emergency and implementing the EAP should be discussed in detail.

Any other special instructions for the dam operators or local officials should be included.

C. Access to the Site
The description of access should focus on primary and secondary routes and means for reaching the site under various conditions, e.g., foot, boat, helicopter, snowmobile. The expected response (travel) time also should be discussed in detail. Special attention should be given to access if the main access road crosses the downstream channel and could be closed by flood waters.

D. Response During Weekends and Holidays
Discussion of emergency response during weekends and holidays should be addressed.

The actions to be taken should be described in detail. Actions should be based on the dam tender schedule for attendance during this period.

Any special procedures for contacting or notifying personnel should be described.

E. Response During Periods of Adverse Weather

Discussion of emergency response under adverse weather conditions should be included.

The actions to be taken should be described in detail. Action should be based on whether the dam is attended or unattended.

Methods of access to the site, *e.g.*, foot, boat, snowmobile, should be described. The expected response time should be discussed in detail.

Any other special instructions for the dam operators or local officials should be listed.

F. Alternative Systems of Communication

The description of the availability and use of alternative communications systems at the site should be included.

Alternative channels of communication to be used in case of failure of the primary system or failure of other systems immediately available should be listed. Proper procedures for activating the alternative channels of communication should be described.

Any other special instructions should be included.

G. Emergency Supplies and Information

There are certain planning and organizational measures that can help the dam owner and local officials manage the emergency situation more safely and effectively. These measures include stockpiling materials and equipment for emergency use and coordinating information. Alternative sources of power for spillway gate operation and other emergency uses also should be provided. The EAP should list the location of each power source, its mode of operation and, if portable, the means of transportation and routes to be followed. The EAP should include the name and day/night telephone numbers of each operator or other responsible person.

If any of these measures apply, they should be discussed in the EAP. Specific types of information to include when describing these emergency supplies and information follow.

1. Stockpiling Materials and Equipment. Where applicable, document the following:

- Materials needed for emergency repair and their location, source, and intended use. Materials should be as close as possible to the dam site.

- Equipment to be used, its location, and who will operate it.

- How the operator or contractor is to be contacted.

- Any other people who may be needed, *e.g.*, laborers, engineers, and how they are to be contacted.

Also include any other special instructions. If stockpiling of materials and equipment is not applicable to your dam, that fact should be stated in your EAP.

NOTE: *For each applicable item, include specific contacts and their business and non-business means of communication.*

2. Coordination of Information. Where applicable, describe the following:

- The need for coordination of information on flows based on weather and runoff forecasts and failure and other emergency conditions. Describe how the coordination is achieved and the chain of communications, including names and day/night telephone numbers of responsible people. Coordination with the NWS or other appropriate agency is recommended to monitor storms, river stages, and flood waves resulting from a dam break. The NWS or other appropriate agency may also be able to supplement the warnings being issued by using its own communication system.

- Additional actions contemplated to respond to an emergency situation or failure at an unattended dam. Include periods of darkness, inclement weather, and non-business hours.

- Actions to be taken to lower the reservoir water surface elevation, if applicable. Describe when and how this action should be taken. If not applicable, that fact should be stated in the EAP.

- Actions to be taken to reduce inflow to the reservoir from upstream dams or control structures. The EAP should provide instructions for operators or other persons responsible for contact with other owners on when and how these actions should be taken. If such actions do not apply, that fact should be stated in the EAP.

- Actions to be taken to reduce downstream flows, such as increasing or decreasing outflows from downstream dams or control structures on the waterway on which the dam is located or its tributaries. The EAP should provide instructions for operators or other responsible persons on when and

27

how these actions should be taken. If such actions do not apply, that fact should be stated in the EAP.

Also describe any other appropriate actions to be taken. If coordination of information on flows is not applicable, that fact should be stated in the EAP.

3. Other Site-Specific Actions
Describe any other site-specific actions devised to moderate or alleviate the extent of possible emergencies.

VII. Inundation Maps
Inundation maps are necessary and should be developed by the dam owner in coordination with the appropriate state and local emergency management agencies. Because those agencies will rely heavily on the maps during an emergency, it is important that the maps contain information required by those agencies. The requirements for an inundation map follow.

The antecedent flow conditions on which the maps are based should be identified. Many local emergency management and response organizations request maps showing both a "sunny day" failure condition and a flood failure condition to show the expected extremes in peak water surface elevations, travel times, and distances downstream between the two scenarios. (For a further discussion see Section VIII.C. - Investigation and Analyses of Dam Break Floods.)

Describe how the inundation boundaries were plotted. At a minimum, show on the map and/or in a table the peak discharge, maximum inundation elevation, and the travel time (in hours and minutes) of the leading edge and peak of the dam break flood wave to critical locations.

The map should be developed at a scale sufficient to be used for identifying downstream inhabited areas within the area subject to possible danger. Inundated areas should be clearly identified. It may be appropriate to supplement the inundation on the maps with water surface profiles showing the elevation before failure, the peak water surface elevation after failure, and the location of structures at critical locations.

A narrative description of the areas affected by the dambreak can be included to clarify unusual conditions. It should describe the specific area threatened and include information on the size and depth of expected flooding relative to known landmarks and historical flood heights. Whenever possible, major streets, railroads, and other well known features should be depicted, using local names or terms.

The best available topographic map should be used. The expected inundation following the assumed failure should be delineated on the map. The lines delineating the inundated area should be drawn in such thickness or form (solid line, dashed line, dotted line) as to readily identify the inundation limits as the main features of the map but not bold enough to obliterate houses or other features which are to be shown as being inundated by the flood waters. Clarity is important. When plotting inundation limits between cross sections used for analysis, the lines should reasonably reflect the change in water levels, with consideration given to topographic patterns and both natural and manmade features. When inundation lines enter the area of an existing lake or reservoir, they should be drawn to represent an increase in the water level of the lake or reservoir. Should this increased water level overtop the dam, the appropriate inundation lines should be drawn downstream of the dam to represent expected inundation in the downstream channel up to a point where an increase in water level will no longer represent danger to life or property. The area between the inundation lines representing the water level may be shaded to distinguish the area of inundation. Care should be taken to select a shading which will not obliterate the background information shown on the map.

The accuracy and limitation of the information supplied on the inundation maps and how best to use the maps should be described. Because local officials are likely to use the maps for evacuation purposes, a note should be included on the map to advise that because of the method, procedures, and assumptions used to develop the flooded areas, the limits of flooding shown and flood wave travel times are approximate and should be used only as a guideline for establishing evacuation zones. Actual areas inundated will depend on actual failure or flooding conditions and may differ from areas shown on the maps. The owner should review the inundation maps with the local jurisdictions and resolve any problems.

If inundation maps are to be shown on several pages, a map index should be included to orient the individual pages.

Inundation maps should be updated periodically to reflect changes in downstream areas.

Include any other pertinent information as a result of coordination with the appropriate emergency management authorities. Emergency management agencies may request that inundation maps highlight evacuation routes and emergency shelters.

VIII. Appendices
Following the main body of the EAP (the basic EAP), an appendix section should be included that contains information that supports and supplements the basic EAP.

Listed below are some of the topics that should be covered in the appendix accompanying the EAP.

- Investigation and Analyses of Dambreak Floods
- Plans for Training, Exercising, Updating, and Posting the EAP
- Site-Specific Concerns
- Approval of the EAP

Each of the these topics are described below.

A. Investigation and Analyses of Dam Break Floods

The EAP appendix should identify and briefly describe the method and assumptions selected to identify the potentially inundated areas.

Several factors usually have to be evaluated whenever dam failures are postulated. The type of dam and the mechanism which could cause failure require careful consideration if a realistic breach is to be assumed. Size and shape of the breach, time of breach formation, hydraulic head, and storage in the reservoir contribute to the dam failure hydrograph. Most of the methods for estimating dam break hydrographs require the choice of size, shape, and time of dam breach. There are also several available procedures for routing dam failure hydrographs to determine information on areas inundated by the flood as it travels downstream.

Several different assumptions on inflow conditions should be made regarding the appropriate conditions prevailing at the time of a dam failure to ensure that the EAP includes all communities that need to be notified. A "fair weather" (often referred to as "sunny day") dam failure (reservoir at normal full pool elevation, normal stream flow prevailing) is generally considered to have the most potential for loss of human life, primarily due to the element of surprise. A failure at the inflow design flood is considered to show the upper limit of inundation.

A failure of a dam during flood flow conditions will result in flooding downstream areas to higher elevations than during a "fair weather" failure. The result could be additional populations and areas affected than otherwise would not occur during a "fair weather" failure. In addition, emergency management agencies may use the inundation maps to develop their evacuation procedures. To assist these agencies, both the "fair weather" breach and a failure during a flood level approaching the inflow design flood (IDF) should be analyzed. If inundated areas for the "fair weather" breach and the IDF breach are essentially the same or are too close to be shown separately on the inundation maps, then a single inundation area for the two breach conditions may be shown. Otherwise, both the "fair weather" breach and the IDF breach should be clearly shown on the inundation map because emergency management agencies advise that they depend on the maps to implement an evacuation and, therefore, need both the "fair weather" and the extreme flood dam failure boundaries shown on the maps.

Many methods for developing the dam failure hydrograph and routing dambreak flows downstream are available. Many federal agencies have developed dambreak computer programs that are available upon request. They may be obtained from the NWS, Bureau of Reclamation, Natural Resources Conservation Service, U.S. Army Corps of Engineers, Tennessee Valley Authority, U.S. Geological Survey, and the Federal Emergency Management Agency. The dambreak model developed by the NWS is the most widely used and preferred.

Sensitivity analyses are recommended to fully investigate the effect of a failure on downstream areas.

The need to consider the domino effect should be made on a case-by-case basis. If the assumed failure of a dam would cause the failure of any downstream dams, the dam owner has the responsibility to consider the domino effect in its routing of the floodwave downstream. The flood wave should be routed to the point where it no longer presents a hazard to downstream life or property, which includes downstream dams. Therefore, the owner, after assuming a hypothetical failure of its dam, should make an engineering judgment regarding the potential for failure of the downstream dams from the flow condition under consideration, or as a result of the failure of the dam being investigated, to determine whether it would be prudent to consider failure of any downstream dams during the routing of the dambreak flood wave.

B. Plans for Training, Exercising, Updating, and Posting the EAP. Plans should be developed for the annual training of project operators and other responsible personnel for conducting periodic EAP exercises, for ensuring timely updating of the EAP, and for posting the notification flowchart.

1. Training. Training of people involved in implementation of the EAP should be conducted to ensure that they are thoroughly familiar with all elements of the plan, the availability of equipment, and their responsibilities and duties under the plan.

Technically qualified personnel should be trained in problem detection and evaluation and appropriate remedial (emergency and non-emergency) measures. This training is essential for proper evaluation of developing situations at all levels of responsibility which, initially, is usually based on on-site observations. A sufficient number of people should be trained to ensure adequate coverage at all times.

A training plan could be included in the appendix to the EAP. Exercises simulating emergency conditions are excellent mechanisms for ensuring readiness. Cross-training in more than one responsible position for each individual is advisable to provide alternates. A careful record by roster should be kept of training completed and refresher training conducted.

2. Exercising. A proposed exercise schedule and the plans for the EAP exercise program should be included in this portion of the appendix. It should also discuss plans for conducting an evaluation of the exercise (both annual drills and periodic comprehensive exercises) and plans for updating the EAP based on the comments from the evaluation.

This section should also include a form that can be used to document actions taken during any actual emergencies.

The state of training and readiness of key personnel responsible for actions during an emergency should be a part of any exercise to make sure that they know and understand the procedures to be followed and actions required.

Any special procedures required for night time, weekends, and holidays should be included. The exercises should involve an annual drill as well as periodic tabletop and functional exercises. Testing of remote sensing equipment at unattended dams should be included.

Coordination and consultation with state and local emergency management officials and other organizations when developing a comprehensive EAP exercise program are important to enhance the realism of the exercises. Their involvement will help perfect the close coordination necessary for a successful execution of emergency procedures in the EAP during an actual emergency. The exercises should include participation by both the dam owner and the affected state and local emergency management officials. The exercises should be evaluated both orally and in writing and the EAP should be revised to correct any deficiencies noted.

3. Updating. The EAP should be updated promptly after each change in involved personnel or their telephone numbers, or after completion of a scheduled exercise.

A review of the adequacy of the EAP should be conducted at intervals not to exceed 1 year. During the review, an evaluation of any changes in flood inundation areas, downstream developments, or in the reservoir should be made to determine whether any revisions to the current EAP (including inundation maps) are necessary.

Reviews should be conducted on or about the same date each year. If no revision is necessary, a statement that the review was made and no revision to the EAP was necessary should be provided to each recipient of the original EAP.

Copies of any revisions that do result from updating the EAP or from periodic exercises of the EAP should be furnished to all individuals to whom the original EAP was distributed. A procedure should be established to ensure that all copies of the EAP are revised. This section should include a list of all recipients of the EAP and should state whether they have the complete EAP (appendices included) or have elected for the basic EAP.

4. Posting of the Notification Flowchart. An up-to-date copy of the notification flowchart should be posted in prominent locations at the dam site and local emergency operations center (essential for unattended dams), as appropriate.

The flowchart should be posted at each phone and radio transmitter at the dam, powerhouse (if applicable), and at all other desirable locations. The locations of the posted flowcharts should be indicated in the EAP.

A copy of the complete, up-to-date EAP should also be available to personnel at the dam and to local officials. The location of each copy should be stated in this section of the EAP. Consideration should also be given to having a copy of the EAP at the residences of key personnel.

C. Site-Specific Concerns
Each dam and downstream area is unique. As a result, each EAP is unique. This section of the appendix should provide a discussion of any site-specific concerns that provide valuable information affecting the EAP. The EAP should emphasize where appropriate structural drawings and flood data are maintained on-site. Quick access to this information is crucial during emergency events.

D. Approval of the EAP
The EAP should include a section that is signed by all parties involved in the plan, where they indicate their approval of the plan and agree to their responsibilities for its execution. Including approval signatures helps to assure that all parties are aware of and understand the EAP and agree to their assigned roles should an emergency occur.

III. GLOSSARY

For the purpose of these guidelines the following definitions apply.

Breach: An opening through the dam resulting in partial or total failure of the dam.

Comprehensive EAP Exercise: An in-depth exercise of an EAP that involves the interaction of the dam owner with the state and local emergency management agencies in a stressful environment with time constraints. Functional and full scale EAP exercises are considered comprehensive EAP exercises.

EAP Exercise: An activity designed to promote emergency preparedness; test or evaluate EAPs, procedures, or facilities; train personnel in emergency management duties; and demonstrate operational capability. Exercises consist of the performance of duties, tasks, or operations very similar to the way they would be performed in a real emergency. However, the exercise performance is in response to a simulated event.

Consequences: Potential loss of life or property damage downstream of a dam caused by floodwaters released at the dam or by waters released by partial or complete failure of dam. Includes effects of land slides upstream of the dam on property located around the reservoir.

Dam Failure: Catastrophic type of failure characterized by the sudden, rapid, and uncontrolled release of impounded water. It is recognized that there are lesser degrees of failure and that any malfunction or abnormality outside the design assumptions and parameters which adversely affect a dam's primary function of impounding water is properly considered a failure. Such lesser degrees of failure can progressively lead to or heighten the risk of a catastrophic failure. They are, however, normally amendable to corrective action.

Emergency Alert System: A federally established network of commercial radio stations that voluntarily provide official emergency instructions or directions to the public during an emergency.

Emergency Management Agency: The state and local agencies responsible for emergency operations, planning, mitigation, preparedness, response, and recovery for all hazards. Names of emergency management agencies may vary such as: Division of Emergency Management, Comprehensive Emergency Management, Disaster Emergency Services, Civil Defense Agency, Emergency and Disaster Services.

Emergency Operations Center (EOC): The location or facility where responsible officials gather during an emergency to direct and coordinate emergency operations, to communicate with other jurisdictions and with field emergency forces, and to formulate protective action decisions and recommendations during an emergency.

Flood Hydrograph: A graph showing, for a given point on a stream, the discharge, height, or other characteristic of a flood with respect to time.

Flood Routing: A process of determining progressively over time the amplitude of a flood wave as it moves past a dam or downstream to successive points along a river or stream.

Hazard Potential: A situation which creates the potential for adverse consequences such as loss of life, property damage, or other adverse impacts. Impacts may be for a defined area downstream of a dam from flood-waters released through spillways and outlet works of the dam or waters released by partial or complete failure of the dam. They may also be for an area upstream of the dam from effects of backwater flooding or effects of landslides around the reservoir perimeter.

Headwater: The water immediately upstream from a dam. The water surface elevation varies due to fluctuations in inflow and the amount of water passed through the dam.

Inflow Design Flood: The floodflow above which the incremental increase in water surface elevation due to failure of a dam or other water impounding structure is no longer considered to present an unacceptable threat to downstream life or property. The flood hydrograph used in the design of a dam and its appurtenant works particularly for sizing the spillway and outlet works and for determining maximum temporary storage, height of dam, and freeboard requirements.

Inundation Map: A map delineating areas that would be flooded as a result of a dam failure.

Notification: To inform appropriate individuals about an emergency condition so they can take appropriate action.

Tailwater: The water immediately downstream from a dam. The water surface elevation varies due to fluctuations in the outflow from the structures of a dam. Tailwater monitoring is an important consideration because a failure of a dam will cause a rapid rise in the level of the tailwater.

www.lightningsource.com/pod-product-compliance
Lightning Source LLC
Chambersburg PA
CBHW080625290526
45790CB00007B/2933